Bubbles

Phil Gates

D1232371

CAMBRIDGE
UNIVERSITY PRESS

Cambridge Reading

General Editors
Richard Brown and Kate Ruttle

Consultant Editor
Jean Glasberg

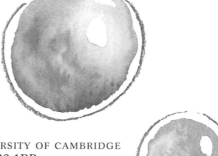

PUBLISHED BY THE PRESS SYNDICATE OF THE UNIVERSITY OF CAMBRIDGE
The Pitt Building, Trumpington Street, Cambridge CB2 1RP

CAMBRIDGE UNIVERSITY PRESS
The Edinburgh Building, Cambridge CB2 2RU, United Kingdom
40 West 20th Street, New York, NY 10011-4211, USA
10 Stamford Road, Oakleigh, Melbourne 3166, Australia

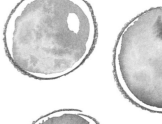

Bubbles
Text © Phil Gates 1996
Illustrations © Jan Lewis 1996

First published 1996
Reprinted 1997

Printed in the United Kingdom at the University Press, Cambridge

A catalogue record for this book is available from the British Library

ISBN 0 521 49933 X paperback

Picture Research: Maureen Cowdroy

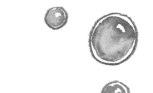

Acknowledgements

We are grateful to the following for permission to reproduce photographs:

Front cover, Comstock Photo Library © 1992 Comstock.
Back cover, Ardea London Ltd (photo: June I MacKinnon).

British Antarctic Survey, 16t (photo: R Price); © Britstock-IFA, 4 (photo: Heinz Koch), 21 (photo: © P Grahammer); John Cleare-Mountain Camera Picture Library, 18l (photo: © Colin Monteath at Mountain Camera, 18r (photo: © John Cleare); Colorific, 5t (photo: Phillip Hayson); Robert Harding Picture Library, 12t, 13, 19 (photo: © William Warren); Helen Hill, 16b; The Image Bank, *title page*, 15t (photo: Juan Pablo Lira), 17b (photo: Brett Froomer); Life File, 9 (photo: Richard Powers), 11b (photo: Mike Potter); Natural History Photographic Agency, 10 (photos: © Stephen Dalton), 14 (photo: © Stephen Dalton); Oxford Scientific Films, 17t (photo: © David Fleetham); © Graham Portlock ABIPP, 5b; Science Photo Library, 20 (photo: NASA/Science Photo Library), 22t (photo: NASA/Custom Medical Stock Photo), 22b (photo:NASA/Science Photo Library), 23t, 23bl (photo: Peter Menzel); Frank Spooner Pictures, 23br (photo: © Gamma); Tony Stone Images, 6 (photo: Jo Browne/Mick Smee), 11t (photo: Suzanne & Nick Geary), 15b (photo: Steve Bly); Telegraph Colour Library, 7, 12b.

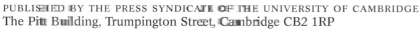

Contents

Have you ever blown a soap bubble
and watched it float away?

A soap bubble has a thin, tight skin which is made of soap and water. The soap bubble is full of air.

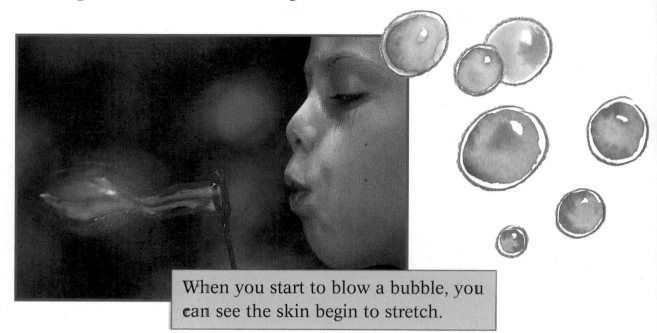

When you start to blow a bubble, you can see the skin begin to stretch.

The bubble's soapy skin is so thin that you can burst it with your finger.

Making soap bubbles

1 Make soap bubbles by pouring some washing-up liquid into a bowl of warm water.

2 Stir the water around quickly until there are lots of bubbles.

3 Then put your ear close to the bubbles. Can you hear the popping noise as their tight skins burst?

Blowing soap bubbles

A bubble is made by trapping air inside
a skin.

When you blow a soap bubble from
a loop you start with a flat, soapy skin.

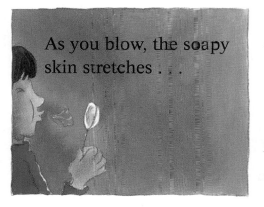

As you blow, the soapy
skin stretches . . .

the skin bulges out . . .

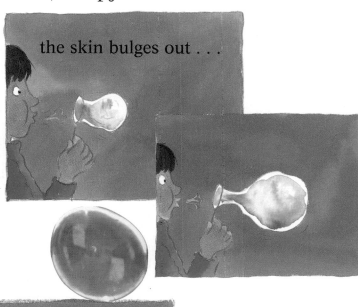

the skin comes off the loop . . .
the hole closes up . . .

and the soapy skin pulls tight.
At last you have made a bubble.

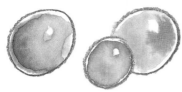

Can you blow square bubbles?

Ask an adult to help you make some loops from wire. Make a round loop and a square loop.

1 Dip each loop in the washing-up liquid.

2 Blow some bubbles with each loop.

3 The round loop should make round bubbles. Does the square loop make square bubbles?

Balloons

Some kinds of bubbles have thicker skins than soap bubbles.

A balloon is a bubble of air with a tight rubber skin.

The skin of a balloon is too strong to burst easily with your finger. You can burst it with something which has a sharp point, like a needle.

When a balloon bursts it makes a loud "bang"!

Thick skins are strong enough to trap
air in many different shapes.

Bouncing bubbles

A bouncy castle is a giant bubble with a very strong plastic skin.

When you jump on this big bubble, you squash the air that is trapped inside the skin.

The air cannot get out through the skin, so it pushes you back up again.

This ball is a kind of bubble. It is full of air and it has a very strong plastic skin.

How does a ball bounce?

1 Throw a ball against a wall.

2 When it hits the wall, the air inside the ball is squashed...

3 but the squashed air pushes back against the wall...

4 so the ball bounces back to you.

Floating bubbles

Bubbles float because the air that is trapped inside them is lighter than water.

Try this

1

Find an empty plastic bottle. (The bottle is not really empty, it is full of air.) Screw the lid on tightly to keep the air in.

2

Put the bottle in a bowl of water.

3

Try to push the bottle under water. Can you feel the water pushing back, making the bottle float?

These armbands are bubbles.
They are full of air and have a
thick plastic skin. They help
children to stay afloat when
they are learning to swim.

This large bubble has a very thick skin.
It is shaped like a boat and is big enough
to carry several people across the water.

Bubbles under water

We need air to breathe. We can breathe the air that is trapped inside a bubble.

If we want to swim under water for a long time then we must take air with us.

We can take air under water inside a kind of bubble. The bubble must have a very strong skin. This diver carries air inside a bottle which has a very strong metal skin.

People can travel under water inside a submarine. A submarine is like a long bubble with a very thick metal skin.

People can live inside a submarine because they can breathe the air inside it.

Above the clouds

There is less air to breathe at the top of
a mountain than there is at the bottom.
  At the top of a very high mountain,
people often breathe air from a bubble.

Mountaineers find it harder to breathe
as they climb higher. When mountaineers
climb a very high mountain they often
carry metal bottles full of air to breathe.

High above the clouds, there is even less air to breathe than at the top of a mountain.

We can fly high in the sky if we travel inside a bubble. An aeroplane is like a huge metal bubble full of air.

Bubbles in Space

There is no air to breathe in Space.

Astronauts must take air with them when they travel into Space. They travel inside a spacecraft, which is like a metal bubble full of air.

The first people to land on the Moon travelled inside the spacecraft Apollo 11.

Astronauts carry metal bottles full of air to breathe – just like the underwater diver and the mountaineer.

Some day, people might live on the Moon. They would have to live inside huge bubbles of air.

The surface of the Moon looks like this.

Scientists have already started to invent
bubbles that people might be able to live in.

A huge bubble has been built on
Earth to see if people, animals
and plants could live inside it for
a long time. This experiment is
called the Biosphere Project.

Index

 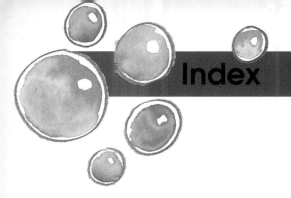
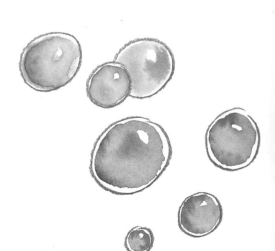